Marriage 21

A Journey Towards Freedom & Deeper Connections

Revs. Myca & Dave Belknap

1. All Scripture referenced is from the King James Version unless otherwise noted.
2. The Mirror Bible. By Francois Du Toit. © 2012 by Mir-rorword Publishing.
3. NIV, The Holy Bible, New International Version. Grand Rapids: Zondervan House, 1984. Print.
4. NKJV, New King James Version. Scripture taken from the New King James Version®. Copyright © 1982 by Thomas Nelson. Used by permission.

All rights reserved.

© 2020 Firebrands 616
Firebrands 616 Ministries Publishing

www.firebrands616.com
cover design, layout & editing by Dave Belknap

Table of Contents

I. Introduction 5
1. Ride the Roller-Coaster 9
2. The Trick Trouble with Trust 15
3. Who's Your Daddy? 21
4. Pay Me Now, Pay Me Later 27
5. Do You See What I See? 33
6. Marriage...Where Ego Goes to Die . .39
7. Great Expectations 45
8. Honesty & Transparency 51
9. "Help-meet" not "Place-mat" 55
10. It Takes Two .61
11. Mama Said 65
12. Mirror, Mirror 71
13. Abra-Ca-Dabra 77
14. There Can Be Only One 83
15. Love is a Battlefield 89
16. Build This Thing Together 95
17. Let's Talk 101
18. Help...is a Two-Way Street 109
19. Only One Call Away 115
20. Waiting on You 121
21. Reminiscing .125

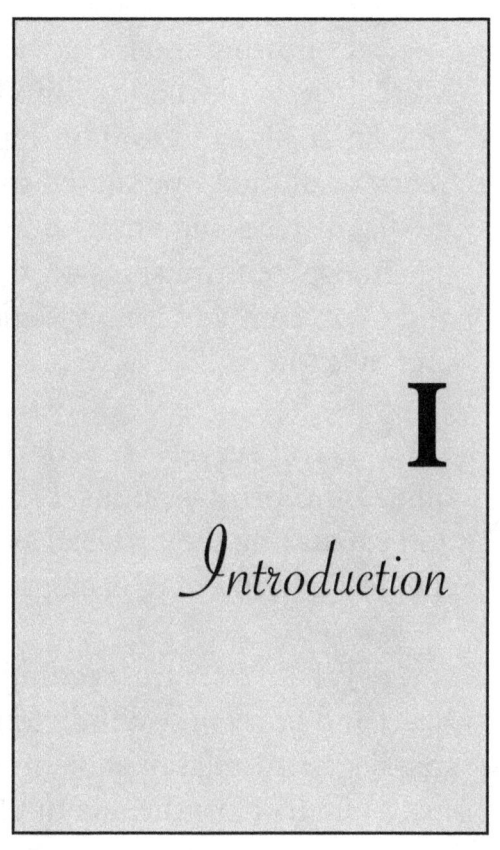

Following their 21st wedding anniversary, Myca began journaling on things she learned about marriage and relationships. As part of a New Years' resolution, she shared sound bites on social media, discovering other couples were blessed by her transparent musings on the beautiful, messy, and often complex factors building two lives into one calls for.

Dave served as editor-in-chief for the digital and print editions, blending his thoughts, and expanding the material as it best served both the flow and intent of each part of the journey.

What you are reading comes from the heart and unity of two individuals who want your marriage and relationships to grow and flourish, just as theirs have throughout life together.

No two couple's journeys are the same. Each marriage is unique, but we hope that in sharing portions of our journey, you are encouraged in yours. Life isn't always a piece of cake, and a good marriage relationship can be a source of strength, hope, and safety.

Marriage can also be challenging. Two imperfect people still in the process of personal growth are not going to be ideal company at every moment of life. It is our hope, and our prayer, that in sharing the good and beautiful things, alongside the messy and difficult we might all be encouraged that at the end of the day love is worth it.

Enjoy the reading and re-reading of this. Following your initial read-through, we encourage you to do so again. But, don't read it front-to-back. Read it out of order. Skip around. You might be surprised as your thoughts while doing so make new connections, and best of all, a greater awareness of yourself and your spouse comes into view.

-Myca & Dave

Do nothing out of selfish ambition or vain conceit. Rather, in humility value others above yourselves, Not looking to your own interests but each of you to the interests of the others.

1

Ride the Roller-Coaster

-(Phillipians 2:3-4, NIV)

A good day or a bad day being married is only one expectation away. As a couple we journey through life together. Often it is easy to get frustrated with our spouse whenever they do or don't do something, and it causes our day or routine inconvenience. Inadvertently, we adopt the mindset that our spouse is supposed to behave in a way that benefits at all times.

It could be little things; how she squeezes the toothpaste tube, where he leaves his dirty clothes, lost car keys, which one of us will do dishes the umpteenth time in a row. These irritants can be the start of arguments, or at least internal grumblings, that really are not necessary. Differences which once fed attraction to each other slowly become irritants when the focus shifts from blessing and serving our soul-mate to survival mode (a.k.a. "Meet my needs and I'll meet yours").

Some expectations must be discussed, agreed upon, and re-visited from time to time as life circumstances are ever changing.

Those expectations are the "big things" like handling of finances, having children, disciplining children, and what each person is comfortable with in the bedroom. These are more obvious and not the ones that are being focused on in this chapter. If I set out expecting my happiness to come from my spouse, my needs to be met, and insecurities to be healed by them I have set both of us up for a roller coaster ride. Not only is any human being incapable of consistently filling that role; but, also I am making my spouse my God. This is a recipe for disaster. Soon as you make anything or anyone an idol, God will make that thing or person fail your expectations in epic proportion!

By contrast, if I approach my spouse with a servant's heart, desiring to be a blessing, I find I am always celebrated and adored. The frustration levels concerning them diminish greatly, and I begin to perceive all the good things my spouse does as gifts: free and undeserved. This brings my life companion into the same focus; a true gift in my life. Someone I am unable to imagine walking through life without.

The law of sowing and reaping kicks in: I meet their needs, mine are met. I bring my spouse joy, I am filled with joy. I ease and heal my spouse's insecurities and mine fade away as well.

James 5:16 says "Confess your faults one to another and pray for each other and you will be healed. The effective, fervent prayer of a righteous person avails much [Myca's paraphrase]." When my approach is vulnerability and gratitude, my expectation brings mutual healing, and my posture is open. I can face conflicts, disappointments, and difficulty with grace.

No relationship is without it's conflicts and irritants. When I operate from a posture of vulnerability and openness, believing the best of my spouse, I am working with God, and even perceived shortcomings and failures turn into successes. Now those are part of a greater journey than simply, and selfishly, meeting culture-given insatiable needs.

When I come from the position of selfless service, gratitude, and non-judgmental love, I am able to have honest, non-threatening conversations with my spouse. We then can address the actions, attitudes, and behaviors that bother each other and hurt our relationship. I can address them with compassion and understanding, and the healing that needs to happen can commence.

Call to Love

Take some time to contemplate the following questions:

What are my expectations concerning my spouse?

Have you talked about the "big ticket items" like money, children/child rearing, and home responsibilities?

In what ways have I set myself and my spouse up for failure?

Write a list of all the wonderful, considerate, and/or helpful things your spouse has done lately.

Find a way to show your gratitude and celebrate those things openly so that your spouse is uplifted.

Not being honest with your spouse is like not being honest with yourself.

2

The Tricky Trouble with Trust

Something to Consider

Trust is a fragile commodity in a world full of scarcity. It requires vulnerability and is risky business. This is the cornerstone of every good relationship. Without trust the most passionate relationships will fizzle out and die.

God started talking to me about marriage while I was quite young. My earliest memory of marriage lessons with the Holy Spirit was when I was 13 years old. Children tend to watch their parents and form opinions about marriage (among other things). They are based on interpretation of how mom and dad walk out their public relationship. As a missionary kid, I felt like I had a front row seat to a variety of couples. I was that kid who no one noticed was around and overheard way too many conversations I shouldn't have. I would watch the couples around me interact and hold an internal conversation: "I don't want that in my marriage!" - and - "I like the way this works in this relationship ... " and so on.

As with most children, I only had a superficial part of the story. I formed opinions, made judgments about something I couldn't possibly understand, and for which I did not have all the facts. Like it or not this is human nature. Unless we are intentional, it is what we will continue to do in all our relationships.

In those early years I was in a "watch and learn" phase. I remember when the Holy Spirit began to talk to me at age 18 about marriage. That it was God's desire for me. I remember saying: "But, I don't want to trade! We've got a good thing going, and I don't have any trouble getting along with You, Lord!"

Leave it to God to use marriage to make me deal with my egocentricity, trust, and abandonment issues! Growing up as a missionary kid meant moving around a lot. As a minister's child it also meant that people came and went from my life. The only constants were my parents. I had learned from experience that no one (outside my immediate family) was willing to stay in my life "through thick and thin". If I (or my parents) somehow caused any disappointment, they would leave and never look back.

God had a different picture to show me, but first I had to be willing to confront my abandonment issues. At the end of all my excuses, fears, reasonings, and rants, the bottom line was that I did not trust God with the "M word".

I reached a new crossroad. Honestly it was a salvation-type experience. I decided that if I could trust my Heavenly Father with my eternity, then I could trust Him with my relationships.

I had to learn to trust God on a whole new level. I embarked on a journey to learn to trust that no matter what happened, no matter what choices my husband might make, and how they might impact my life, my Heavenly Father has His Hand in the journey. I had to trust God has worked out a plan that is for my good. I also had to trust that no matter what I did, God also has my husband's best interest at heart as well, and the two are not mutually exclusive!

Trust is at the foundation of every relationship. Here's what I learned: my trust in my husband is only as strong as my trust in God. Ultimately, it all comes down to trust and surrender.

Call to Love

Take some time today to check your trust levels, both of God and your spouse.

Ask the Holy Spirit to shine a light on one area of yourself personally that you are not trusting God in, and ask the Holy Spirit to give you Divine perspective.

Contemplate ways that you can increase your trust in your spouse.

Ask the Holy Spirit to guide you, and then give each other time and opportunities to grow into that new trust.

*For this reason
I kneel
before the Father,
from whom
every family
in heaven
and on earth
derives its name.*

- *(Ephesians 3:14-15, NIV)*

3
Who's Your Daddy?

Where we come from often overrules our verbally (and internally) professed belief systems. How we behave, how we perceive others, and what we consider to be "common sense" or courtesy has more to do with how we were raised and the individual experiences that formed us than actual "common sense".

What is obvious to one person is only obvious because it is within that person's perception or perspective view of the world. Many a hurt feeling has come from unfulfilled expectations that fall within someone's "common-sense arena". Uncommunicated expectations are never fair to the other person.

What is the source of the romance, joy, and contentment in your marriage? Is it based on what your spouse does (chores, chocolates, roses, date nights)? Most likely, you've developed likes from what you observed (or what was lacking) in your own family. More-so, your experience was at least somewhat different than your spouse's; so, you both probably have different expectations and perceptions of "how a marriage should be".

Communicate to your spouse what it is that makes you feel uniquely loved and appreciated.

If your family model was lacking, it's a good idea to look at healthy examples and the Word of God to begin to build a new picture of the marriage relationship. Biblically speaking, "Abba" (father) is the source from which the family flows and is the source of love, provision, and purpose for the children of the household. Every relationship in your life flows from a source.

Sometimes we form relationships out of need, fear, or our own wounds. Just be careful to not do too much comparing. Every relationship has it's differences and nuances. Ultimately, you and your spouse must agree on what your marriage will look like and how you will meet each other's relational needs.

Do this first: identify the foundation of your relationship. Why did you pursue and fall in love with your spouse? If your relational choices come from your own baggage, then deal with your baggage so that you can tap into the ultimate source of love and romance instead of your fear and pain-based, contaminated well. Then, from time to time, we need little reminders of the blessings that our spouse is to us.

Don't let familiarity extinguish the passion in your relationship! Identifying what it is about your relationship that gives you joy and light your candle, is a key factor in keeping the flame alive in the marriage relationship. Remembering and then focusing on what you love about each other causes the smaller annoyances to fade into the background and results in falling in love with each other all over again. Although your spouse is not supposed to be your "ultimate source", they are to be a source of joy, inspiration, and motivation to become the best version of you possible.

As a minister and a teacher, I encounter a great diversity of family situations. From newly-weds to ugly divorces, and single parents too, the range of relational examples are all over the board. Each new situation I encounter has me running home to my man and appreciating him all the more. Use the "there's always someone worse off" to help you refocus on the things that are working in your relationship and highlight the areas that you love. Then, when you start to work on areas that need improvement you can tackle them from a place of abundance and gratitude, not from a place of lack and criticism.

Call to Love

Make a list of his/her most endearing qualities. Pick one to highlight and celebrate it today.

Choose one day (or week) a month to set aside time to fall in love with your spouse all over again.

Make a point to both tell and show your spouse specifically what it is that you really LOVE about him/her (be specific).

Trust in the Lord with all thine heart; and lean not unto thine own understanding. In all thy ways acknowledge him, and he shall direct thy paths.

4
Pay Me Now, Pay Me Later

-(Proverbs 3:5-6, KJV)

Being married to someone does not mean that you get to stop improving and growing as a human being and a child of God. In fact, sharing your life so intimately can often bring to the surface your greatest areas of need for growth. I really have never liked the saying "marriage is work". It has never felt like my relationship with my spouse is work, but I understand the premise behind the saying. I will add a different perspective to this saying and some qualifications to "work".

First of all, if you are doing something that you love and are passionate about, it will never "seem" like work. You will consider the time, sweat, tears, and effort as a privilege and a joy, not work or a job to be done. Having said that, marriage requires intentionality, selflessness, and the willingness to grow and allow the other person to grow as well.

Second, we must redefine the word "work" for the marriage context. Work, at least in the Western world, has come to mean a necessary toil on the outside. It is something we suffer through in order to be able to afford the activities we are truly passionate about. Seemingly rare is the individual who truly enjoys "work". Sure, many of us find our work "meaningful", and may even enjoy the people we work with/for. But we look forward to a day we do not *have* to work.

Work also implies some kind of external productivity that in some way results in benefiting me or meeting my personal wants, needs, and desires. Work always has an end-date. It is considered temporary and useful only until we reach our "work goals". Marriage "work", as with most relationships occurs largely on the internal field - that is, if the work is going to be successful, the source of the "improvements" must come from within.

The lion's share of the "work" to be done in my marriage is on me. Marriage "work" is ongoing. It never ends. In the beginning, marriage requires that we "grow up" and stop stressing over the "small stuff". It requires us to put our pet peeves and preferences in perspective, and make decisions based on what is good for more than just ourselves. This kind of "work" is the same kind of "work" that we should be doing (whether married or single) as children of God called to reflect His image and likeness.

Marriage requires flexibility. It requires that we synchronize our own personal evolution with the personal evolution of our spouse and find harmony in each other's growth.

Much of that growth process will require that we communicate our wants and needs without being a demanding nag. We also have to be self-aware enough to communicate how we are changing and growing. This requires us to go to new levels of openness and vulnerability. The two must strike a healthy balance between complete acceptance and the tension required to keep each other growing both relationally and as individuals.

Call to Love

Do a self-evaluation. Ask the Holy Spirit to show you an area that you could grow/improve on in your relationship.

Take time to share your discovery with your spouse. Agree on how you would like him/her to help you on your growth journey.

If you have been married for a while, think back on how your spouse has grown as an individual and as a partner.

Make a point to tell your spouse how proud and blessed you are to see all they accomplish.

Greater love has no one than this, than to lay down one's life for his friends.

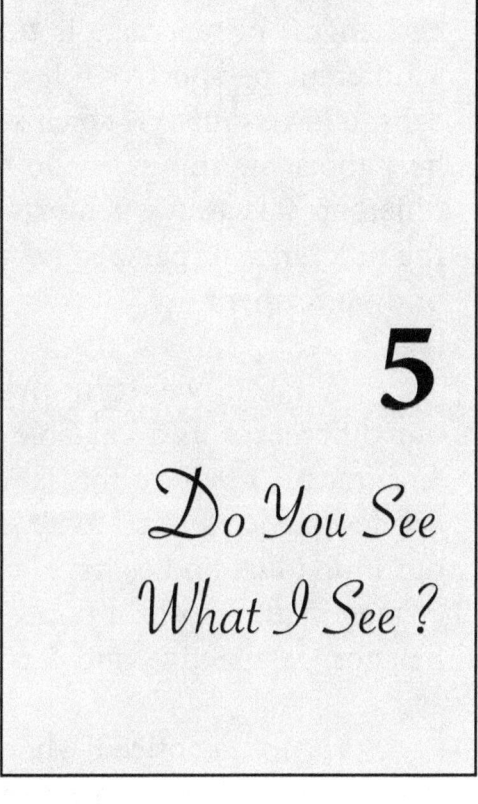

5
Do You See What I See?

- (John 15:13, NKJV)

One of the greatest benefits (and challenges) of marriage is the constant input of a different perspective. It can be hard on our egos to have someone so close to us see and even hear the same things we do yet have an entirely different "takeaway". Unfortunately, often we see the difference of perspective as a lack of support or disagreement.

What if we turn that around and see our differences as a valuable benefit. A kind of "insurance". I believe this is what our differences are designed/intended to be. Think of it this way: our individual bodies have "twos" so that we can engage in the world around us with the proper balance, perspective, and depth perception.

Have you noticed, when the optometrist fits you for glasses, they check each eye individually before checking them together? When both eyes work properly (both individually and in concert) we have depth perception that allows us to perceive the three dimensional world, both far away and up-close. Our hearing functions in a similar way: discerning both detail and directionality. The doctor tests each ear individually. When both ears work together we are able to better discern where sounds come from.

We have two legs in order that we may walk upright. One leg is usually a little stronger than the other; however, if the difference is too great you end up with a host of back problems - it throws off your core. Soon you'll find yourself "limping along". We could continue the metaphor with our two arms and so on, but I think I've made my point.

When we begin to appreciate the differences of both perspectives, we can build on each others' strengths without resorting to restrictive roles. We will also begin to see things more clearly and can engage in life with a greater sense of balance and meaning.

In order to be able to see things from a new perspective we must practice the art of listening, keep an open mind, and grow out of some of our own insecurities. In marriage, there is no room for a control freak. If you must be right all the time or in control of every situation, go get some help.

One of the biggest temptations in marriage is to try to change the things you do not like about your spouse. This is a relationship killer. Instead, learn to lean on each other's strengths and do not allow traditional roles to get in the way of your marriage.

Call to Love

Take a moment to communicate (in both words and deeds) to your spouse that you "hear and see" them.

In addition, take time to let them know you value their differences and appreciate their perspective, enough to prefer theirs over your own.

*Two are better than one,
If either of them falls down,
 one can help the other up.
If two lie down together, they will keep warm.
A cord of three strands is not quickly broken.*

6

Marriage . . . Where Ego Goes to Die

-(excerpts from Ecclesiates 4:9-12, NIV)

The level of trust, vulnerability, and inter-reliance needed for a rich and deep relationship leaves no room for egoism. Transparency and vulnerability require that each person feel safe being who they are both individually and in the relationship. Egoism, selfishness, and "my way is the best way" attitudes are relationship killers. Not to mention annoying and childish. Living through life's ups and downs so closely with another human being has a way of bringing to the surface all our worst qualities.

Marriage is a safe place where we can expose our own egos, deal with them, and practice the art of altruism. Each day gives both small and large scale opportunities to walk in love. From the toothpaste squeezed from the middle, toilet seats left up, spending money we don't have, and dealing with family illnesses and deaths.

Adversity can either divide you or make you stronger. Ego is the key. If you play the blame game, adversity will divide you, create resentment and break down the intimacy you share. If you walk in forgiveness, give each other grace, and pull together to face adversity, your bond will strengthen and your intimacy will deepen.

When Dave and I first married, we would have seasons where checks bounced left and right. I lived on my own for a couple years and was used to using a checking account. Dave operated on a cash-only basis, and what was in hand (or appearing available) was what he worked with. Dave also had the benefit of being able to live in the house he grew up in while it was being renovated (which allowed us to save money before we got married).

Over the years Dave and I have found our financial rhythm, but their were a few stressful moments in which I had to choose to accept the fact that my husband needs time and grace to learn and grow just as I do.

Finances is just one area that can be challenging in a marriage. When we marry, we join ourselves to a human being not an idea or an ideal. As such, grace must be extended for growth, mistakes, bad attitudes, and difficult days. The saying: "A good marriage can be like heaven on earth, but a bad marriage can be like hell on earth" holds true based on the degree to which you each control or yield to your egoistic, selfish natures. Each day, each moment, is a choice and an exercise in either selfishness or selflessness.

Along the way, we get the privilege of a front row seat to watch the Hand of God move another beloved child of God through the journey of their life. It's the closest we will come to truly sharing oneness. We get to share the joy, pain, struggles, and victories in a way that we only experience within ourselves.

Marriage is the ultimate reminder that we are never alone. No one, beside God, will ever be more connected or more intimately acquainted with you, your thoughts, feelings, and nuances than your spouse - if they take the opportunity and if you let them truly see the real you.

Call to Love

Before dealing with the "business of life" make sure that you tell and show your spouse that they are more important than the temporary inconvenience that they may have caused.

Mistakes don't define our value or worth.

Mistakes are merely the learning opportunities on our journey of life.

*Settle it
in your heart:
your marriage
is as unique
as the two
of you*

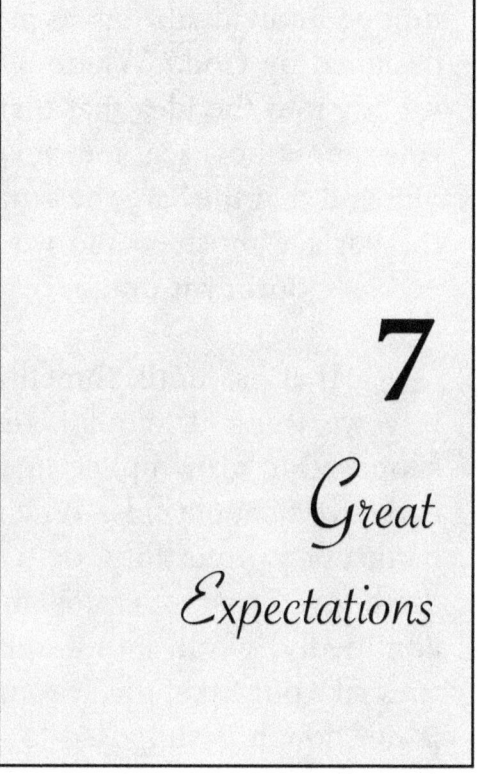

7
Great
Expectations

Something to Consider

Not one of us would argue that we are unique individuals on a personalized journey designed by God. Where it gets tricky is when we buy into the idea that there are hard and fast rules about how that journey is supposed to play out; and that they are the same for everyone. On the surface most people would agree that each person's journey is unique.

That is, until something doesn't go the way we think it should! For example: you're supposed to grow up, get married, buy a house, and have a couple kids. When, suddenly, divorce, bankruptcy, infertility, or a child born with a disability turns your preplanned (though never admittedly) world into a tailspin. At this point we shake our fist at the heavens and declare: "This is not how it is supposed to be!" The statement alone reveals our expectations of sameness.

Our ingrained belief that if we do "the right things" then nothing bad will ever happen to us. We have these preconceived ideas and expectations of every "successful" marriage looking the same as well. We use these expectations to fortify our sense of control and to manipulate others into playing the game the way we want it to be played. Settle it in your heart: your marriage is as unique as the two of you!

Your parents' marriage may have been the roll model you had; however, you are not your parents neither are you marrying your spouse's parents. And, while we are at it, you are in control of very little in your life. Least of all other people. Your control extends only to yourself. So, get off the comparison train!

In my parents' relationship, my father was in charge of the finances and although they made decisions together, it seemed (from my "child's perspective") that dad was the instigator and mom usually agreed with him. Dad did the "outside stuff" and mom did the "inside stuff". There were clearly defined roles that worked quite well for them.

Culture and years of Evangelical traditions have created unspoken expectations for couples in all areas of life. What if your husband is weak in managing finances? Traditional roles say he'll learn and just trust God to make up the difference.

After a couple of years living life together, Dave and I realized that neither of us neatly fit into the conventional/traditional marriage rolls. We discovered that if we leaned on each other's strengths we experienced a greater peace in our relationship, less stress, and greater levels of trust. This showed true in each other, and in God working all things for good in our individuality and marriage relationship.

Like the old proverb I remember fondly, "The road we walk is paved with stones that bruise our feet." The point being that our very journey is made up of both moments of pain and of progress. Often pain is the vehicle of progress. We can either go through the ups and downs of life as a united front or allow them to divide us. It's a choice.

Call to Love

Take a moment to examine your expectations both of yourself and your spouse.

Ask the Holy Spirit to reveal to you any undisclosed and/or unrealistic expectations that are sabotaging your marriage.

What seems "common sense" to one person is not so common to another, including spouses.

Ask the Holy Spirit to reveal to you if your expectations are born out of your own woundedness, egocentricity, or even culture.

*Be kind
and compassionate
to one another,
forgiving
each other,
just as in Christ
God forgave you.*

- (Ephesians 4:32 , NIV)

Honesty, transparency, and vulnerability are the hallmarks of a good marriage. Without those, trust is fleeting. Pettiness takes over, and you find yourselves second guessing each others' motives. Let's face it, though, honesty, transparency, and vulnerability are risky business. When we let someone in to the depths of our hearts we also risk greater pain WHEN they hurt us...and they will hurt us. At some point (hopefully unintentionally) our spouse will do or say something that wounds our hearts. A bad attitude. Words spoken during times of stress, frustration, or exhaustion can pierce like a sword.

When this happens, we have a choice. We can work it out through more (risky) openness, forgiveness, and communication, we can ignore it and suppress our feelings, or we can harbor resentment and unforgiveness. If we harbor resentment and unforgiveness, each consecutive offense carries a cumulative effect. Every time our spouse wounds us interest compounds on the "credit card debt" of our relationship; to the point the debt can never be "worked off with good deeds".

Another option is to suppress our feelings and "ignore" the offense. We may even excuse it away by telling ourselves the words/deeds were spoken/done unintentionally or were "out of the norm" for our spouse. It may even seem so mature and spiritual of us to just "let it go". Now, I'm not saying it's impossible, but usually this is just an avoidance tactic because we fear confrontation and further wounding. If it isn't genuine, we'll find ourselves shutting down just a little bit more each time we "overlook" offenses. Soon, we'll find ourselves having "fallen out of love". Love and relationship are "risky business".

You have heard this saying before, and it is echoed throughout the American culture: "It's better to have loved and lost than to never have loved at all." Though true, sometimes (in the moment) the loss of love seem unbearable... especially when the loss comes in the form of rejection, abandonment, or betrayal. When we say "let's talk", we risk being misunderstood, our pain being minimized, or even more rejection. We also open up the chance not only for reconciliation but also for a deepening of the relationship. It will be uncomfortable at first. However, if we are to grow in our relationship and honor one another, it is vital that even in fear and pain we remain open, tender, and willing to see and value the other in each other.

Marriage isn't fifty-fifty, it's 100/100. Both of you, all in, all the time. There is no room for a "my way or the highway", it has to be an us-or-bust viewpoint in the mentality of both partners.

Call to Love

Share with your spouse what you are going through and how you really feel.

Include your spouse in both your internal and external journey.

Giving thanks to God the Father for everything, in the name of our Lord Jesus Christ. Submit to one another out of reverence for Christ.

9

"*Help-meet*"

not

"*Place-mat*"

- (*Ephesians 5:20-21 , KJV*)

Help-meet, not place-mat...it's easier than you think!

I believe it's only natural that we want to help the people that we love. Each of us approach what that "help" looks like based on our personalities and to some extent, whether we are male or female. Personally, I dislike generalizing based on gender. More often than not, what defines our level of ability to be supportive, helpful in our relationships is more dependent on our experiences and what we took away from them than our gender-based tendencies. Frankly, it rubs me the wrong way when people just assume that a man or woman is limited to feeling or unfeeling solely based on their reproductive organs.

I've always pushed back against gender roles and expectations. As a child, I played with toy guns, rolled in the mud, and was very "rough and tumble" for a "girl". When it comes to marriage, I went back to Genesis where it all began: Gen. 2:18 "Then the LORD God said, "It is not good for the man to be alone; I will make him a helper (*'ezer* is translated *boethos* in the

Greek Septuagint - LXX) suitable for him." The word "helper" (also translated help-meet) is *ezer*, a masculine word and is used to describe God as our helper and is included as part of the names of people throughout the Bible (all males by the way).

The definition of boethos is "one who runs on hearing a cry to give assistance". Thomas Constable says, "the term helper does not mean a servant. Jesus Christ used the same word to describe the Holy Spirit who would help believers following the Lord's ascension ... suitable to him or corresponding to him means "what was true of Adam (cf. Ge 2:7) was also true of Eve". They both had the same nature."- (*From Constable's Expository Notes Online*)

Our culture is one that is constantly trying to determine who's on first. Who is the greatest? Who is in charge? The institution of marriage flies in the face of ego and sets each up for opportunities; both to lead and follow. It is the mystery of Christ and the Church worked out in living color. One of the greatest gifts we can give one another in relationships is to *ezer*... to yield our strength, our resources, our talents, and our wisdom for the sake of the other.

Whether it is husband helping wife, or wife helping husband it makes no difference. To ezer, is to reflect the very nature of God.

If you feel like the doormat in your relationship, the first step is to stop viewing yourself this way! Your spouse has gotten used to the way things are, and you have participated to some degree (I'm not talking about controlling or abusive relationships).

The good news is you are not stuck in this role. Your part in this covenant of love can, and is, allowed to change as you and your spouse mature. Consider the shell of a boiled egg for a moment. It keeps what is inside protected, yet itself is fragile. I propose you allow that shell to crack. Let it slowly break away to reveal the strength that is within.

Call to Love

Ask the Holy Spirit to change your internal view of yourself and then communicate in a blame-free way how you are growing in your own self-worth.

Make a plan with your spouse so that you can begin letting go of some of the things that have made you feel like you are doing it all.

Keep in Mind: It will take time for them to pick up new habits of responsibility, just as it took you time to grow into the person that you are now.

Trust in the Lord with all thine heart; and lean not unto thine own understanding. In all thy ways acknowledge him, and he shall direct thy paths.

-(Proverbs 3:5-6, KJV)

10
It Takes Two

It Takes Two to Make a Thing Go Right! It Takes Two to Make Out-a-sight! The thing about the original design of marriage is that the success of the marriage really does depend on both of you. Neither husband nor wife can carry the whole thing. It's "together or not at all" situation. This can be scary because so much rides on your partner's willingness to be vulnerable, transparent, and most of all both grow and allow you to grow as well.

When it comes to the "design" of marriage, we look to Genesis for an idea of how the two work as one in order to form the "image and likeness" of the creator. The Hebrew words for male and female are *zachar* (רכז) and *nekeva* (הבקנ). *Zachar* means "remember" and *nekeva* roughly means "to look to the horizon (future)". Together they represent "yesterday, today, and forever". This is not meant to be a basis for setting hard and fast rules or rolls in the marriage so as to limit one or the other. Rather, the qualities that are brought together are meant to reflect something that is timeless.

Just as God is from before the beginning, in our present, and encompasses our future, the marriage relationship is meant to reflect a timeless, life-filled, light-giving love that goes beyond history and brims with future hope. If the male dominates, the relationship is stuck in the past and cannot move forward. If the female dominates, all that was is lost and there is nothing to build a future upon.

What this means is that your relationship (the working together) alone has the potential to declare the gospel. Only as we learn to yield, lean on each other's strengths, and refuse to blame or shame each other's weaknesses, will we reflect the image and likeness. How you serve, love, and prefer each other is a living, breathing picture of Christ and the church.

The life (lives) you produce and the lives you impact are a direct response to this glory. The more we yield to one another, honor each other, and resist the urge to fix each other the greater the glory and joy of reflecting God's image and likeness will be seen.

Dave and I have arranged that the one who is either most passionate or most affected by the decision can make the final call. If we are both passionate and equally affected, we don't decide until we can agree. The honoring thing is not always the quickest or the easiest, but no one said marriage was going to be all roses all the time.

Call to Love

Discuss those areas that you are not in agreement with your spouse.

Be willing to see things from their point of view.

After, share how this affects you and how you can both better relate in this area moving forward.

And beside this, giving all diligence, add to your faith virtue; and to virtue knowledge; And to knowledge temperance; and to temperance patience; and to patience godliness;

-(2 Peter 1:5-6 , KJV)

11
Mama Said

Momma said there'd be days like this... Let's face it, no one is perfect and everyone has moments, days, or longer when they behave badly, make bad decisions, and are "off their game".

H. Jackson Brown, Jr said: "Enjoy the satisfaction that comes from doing little things well." Often it's the little things that build up over time that tend to wear down relationships. It's important that we be honest with our spouse about those "pet peeves". A certain level of annoyance is normal in a relationship. It's part of iron sharpening iron as well as part of God's design for helping us master our egos. However, continued irritation combined with a lack of communication can dim those love-flames.

So, take some advice from "wise old" Solomon: "Catch for us the foxes, the little foxes that ruin the vineyards, our vineyards that are in bloom" (Song of Songs 2:15). As a single person, it was easy for me to ignore those moments because for the most part they only affected me...or so I thought.

In the marriage relationship your life is on display pretty much 24/7. Those bad financial decisions that no one else would know about are no longer hidden. The extra "roll" from binge eating to stuff your emotions are evident, and we come face to face with the fact that our decisions are no longer just about us. When we fall into a pit regardless of what shape it takes (financial, food choices, drinking too much, fits of anger, or selfishness...) we have some choices we can make.

How we respond to ourselves (when we have a "bad day") and how we respond to our spouse (when s/he has a "bad day") can either bring shame or healing. If our response is one of judgments and "I told you so", then we will cause more damage. If our response is love, acceptance, and identifying with ourselves and our spouse that these momentary lapses are common to us all, then we can bring about healing in ourselves, our spouse, and our marriage.

The difficult part about extending grace to our spouse is that we struggle with extending grace to ourselves. If you struggle with extending grace to yourself, forgiving yourself, and loving yourself through the "bad days", then you will also struggle with extending that same grace to those closest to you. Those you are closest to (especially a spouse) are "one" with you and you feel the right to expect of them the same standards as you expect of yourself.

If you extend grace to them, then you must also let go of your expectations and extend grace to yourself. However, if you let go of those expectations, then you must accept that you are "enough" aside from your actions. And if you are enough, then your spouse, children, co-workers... everyone is enough, and off the performance hook.

Call to Love

Let your spouse know today they are everything that you ever hoped for and dreamed of.

Be quick in asking forgiveness from them, communicate when you've been hurt, and forgive each other.

*But we all,
with open face
beholding as in
a glass the glory
of the Lord,
are changed into
the same image
from glory to glory,
even as by
the Spirit
of the Lord.*

-*(2 Corinthians 3:18 , KJV)*

12
Mirror Mirror

Mirror, mirror, on the wall...

I recently made some major changes to the way I eat. I didn't start a diet, I changed my lifestyle. As a result of these changes, not only do I feel better, have more energy, and have a clearer mind, but I've also lost a few pounds. Like most of us, I've gone on many diets, and l have lost (and re-gained) more weight than I'd care to admit. Every diet I have gone on was full of temptations, successes and failure, and a general sense of me being "good" or "bad".

This time, I decided on an "un-diet". Instead of adding one more thing to my very busy plate that I must "do" in order to be successful, I decided that I would start making choices based on self-care. Making healthy food choices means making your own well-being a priority. It means that I am "worth" the time it takes to plan and make a healthy meal rather than grab whatever is around to stuff down my throat and silence the hunger. Healthy choices also means taking the time to recognize whether my body needs nourishment or my emotions need attention.

Little did I realize that deciding to take care of me would impact my marriage. Turns out that when we tend to our own garden our spouse (our children, and pretty much anyone else who must tolerate us) benefits from our increased patience, grace, and overall well-being. When I chose to love and accept myself my capacity to both give and receive love increased as well.

Another unexpected benefit was that my resilience to adversity also grew. At the time of this being written Dave's work requires a lot of travel, and rarely has any kind of kitchen to prepare (much less keep) food in. Though he has tried to make some similar changes in his diet as I have, it's been in slower smaller steps. One weekend, we were sitting down at a restaurant eating lunch together and he thanked me for not saying anything about the food he ordered. It spurred a conversation between us about how important it has been in our relationship to avoid the urge to control each other, allowed each other to grow in our own ways and at our own pace, and to support one another without chiding or trying to "parent our spouse".

I also realized that, for the first time in my adult life, I was no longer judging myself for my food choices. Since I wasn't judging me, I felt no need to judge anyone else either. Coincidence? I think NOT! Here again, was an unexpected benefit of my un-diet choice.

The closer the relationship the more the opportunity for our control issues to come out. We tell ourselves it's because we love so deeply that we just want the person (whether spouse, friend, or children) to do what's best for them. Since I am not judging myself based on my diet failures and successes, I find it easier not to judge my spouse while he's figuring this whole thing out. So, when my husband falls off the "healthy eating/lifestyle" wagon he is enough and there is no judgment. I do not require his participation in my decisions to feel his support. Should his meal choices tempt me to eat something that's not in line with my healthy choices, I do not blame him for my cravings. Neither do I judge myself for mindless emotional eating here and there. When I recognize it, then I can deal with whatever is needed. It's not about performance. It's about accepting the fact that I am enough, he is enough, we are enough.

And so are you! Take some time today to celebrate your spouse. Cast all of your anxieties, worries, and control issues (even if just for a moment) into the capable hands of your Loving Father God. Now, look at your spouse through God's eyes. See the magnificent creation, the beautiful soul, and the eternal spirit that has trusted you enough to share life with you. Then, find ways to express that gratitude to your spouse.

Call to Love

Use your words to build up your spouse today.

Let them that they are the best spouse, parent, and friend.

Speak to their dreams, their vision for their life and yours together, and call them into reality.

Your Christ mindedness completes my delight! You co-echoe the same agape; we are soul mates, resonating the same thoughts.

13
Abra-ca-dabra

- (Philippians 2:2
The Mirror Bible)

It seems like magic when things go well in a marriage. Both Dave I grew up hearing songs like *Love Potion #9* and *I Told the Witch-doctor*. Our parents all loved the "oldies but goodies", and regularly subjected their children to their outdated music (So much that Dave is a great source of lyrical trivia). Sometimes a good relationship, not unlike magic, can seem mystical and elusive.

If you did not have parents to model a successful marriage, then it becomes even more difficult to "catch the moves" that are needed to cultivate long, healthy, fulfilling, and lasting relationships. If your parents were extremely private and didn't live "authentically" before their children, it is also difficult because some of the most important marital ingredients remained unseen.

[*NOTE: For this segment, We are staying away from the sexual aspects of marriage.*]

How do people cultivate deep, meaningful, satisfying, and lasting marriage relationships? Aside from the physical attraction piece which is either there or it's not (*or is it?*), what goes into the proverbial stew of marriage magic? I love the phrase *Abra-ca-dabra*. I also love using it with Christians, and for more than the considerable shock value. In Hebrew it loosely means *I create what I speak*. Proverbs tells us that life, and death, "*are in the power of the tongue, and those who love it will eat its fruit* (Proverbs 18:21)." I've highlighted two words in Proverbs 18:21 that I believe are key to unlocking part of the mystery of our relationships.

The words that we say, and how we truly feel about them are important. Let me try to unpack the concept as briefly as possible. We have two voices: an internal voice and an external voice. All of us have an "internal conversation". These conversations happen in our ruminations, and are not just random thoughts.

Our internal conversation is more often honest than our external conversations. We often think one thing and say another. This practice is so normalized that we don't realize how often we do it. For example, our spouse asks: "Do you mind if I stay at work late tonight to finish a few things up?" On the inside you think/say: "Again!? I really need to get away from your children!" Then you reply out-loud: "No problem. I've got things covered here. What time do you think you'll be home?"

The point is, we rarely say what we are really feeling or thinking on the inside, especially if we believe those thoughts/feelings may not be acceptable in some way. Our internal voice is what we "say" to ourselves (also known as "self-talk"), in the privacy of our own thoughts, regardless of social norms and "adult correctness". Our internal thoughts can be a way for us to process a situation and make decisions about what we will do and how we will behave.

Our external voice is what we say aloud to ourselves and others. When the words that we say aloud align with the words that we say in silence then we produce fruit and partake (eat) and experience the results (manifestation) of our words. Similar to the creation story in Genesis, we say "_____ be " and "_____ is" created. The more aligned our words are (external conversation) and feelings (internal conversation + desire) the more "light" we create.

Though I won't focus on the negative in this section please note the same applies to negative words that are aligned with negative emotions. When both our voices are in agreement our words are impactful and they produce an atmosphere that perpetuates what we are reinforcing. When our voices are not in agreement then our message is "mixed" and may sound insincere, condescending, or even offensive. Most of the time, people are not sure why they feel badly or distrustful when we talk to them. We could be saying all the right things. We could be doing all the right things. If our voices are not aligned, all those "right things" fall flat at best, and are interpreted as manipulative, dishonest, or worse.

What you say internally carries the most weight with your spouse and with yourself. Being vulnerable, honest, and open about the feelings and thoughts you are not proud of removes the "mystery" and opens the door for those feelings and thoughts to be addressed, healed, and replaced with what you truly desire.

It takes a great deal of courage to open up and be truly honest in our current social and religious culture of shame, performance, and perfection. We are constantly challenged to self-protect and fight the messages that we are too much _____ or not enough _____.

I'll close with a quote from one of my new favorite songs by Sara Barailles, called *Brave*;

But I wonder what would happen if you - Say what you wanna say - And let the words fall out - Honestly I wanna see you be brave.

Call to Love

Look at your spouse's success .

Begin feeling them as your own...because they are!

Allow yourself to realize when one of you "wins" that victory belongs to both of you.

Be devoted to one another in love. Honor one another above yourselves.

14
There Can Be Only One

- (Romans 12:10, NIV)

In a movie called *Highlander*, a group of super-humans ("Immortals" in the movie's terms) battle each other to the death in order to gain all the essence or power of the quickening. I think sometimes we think that oneness in marriage, like unity in the body means something similar. Only one person could win and the others will be subjugated (hint: it doesn't).

When Dave and I got married there were times when I struggled with thoughts about how God was going to make us one. Dave is spontaneous, pastoral, creative, and messy. I'm an organized planner with a call to the nations. I never doubted that God brought us together. I just wondered what the heck He was thinking! How is this supposed to work? Over the years I've seen that my doubts were just projections of my old religious-trained thoughts mixed with insecurity. I had visions of one or the other of us always having to sacrifice his/her dreams in order for the other to be fulfilled. And, you know what? For many years that is exactly the way it played out!

...Or so I thought.

It turns out there is no such thing as the sidelines in the Kingdom of God or in marriage. Oneness is not about dominance, it's about blending. Each one ministers his/her gift according to grace and by faith. Whether out on the front lines or behind the scenes, who you are is reflective of your deepest and most intimate relationships - marriage included.

When I minister is Latin America, Dave's influence is there with me. When he travels the country training staff, my influence is with him. Our "oneness" grows every year as we learn to yield to one another more and as we come into more agreement, acceptance, and honoring of each other. The more we celebrate both our differences and our agreements the more "one" we become.

In the book of Acts, Priscilla and Aquila operated this way in ministry. Sometimes Priscilla would lead (as noted in her name mentioned first), and other times Aquila would lead. Another noted Bible example happened while Peter and John were at the Gate Beautiful, where the lame man was healed, there is a small yet beautiful clause that most people breeze by: When he saw Peter and John about to enter the temple, he asked them for money. Peter looked directly at him, as did John. "Look at us!" said Peter (Berean Study Bible). Although Peter was doing all the talking, John was engaged as more than an observer. Peter also included John when he said: "Look at US"! So it is with oneness in marriage. There is no "me". There is only us.

I'm not the same individual I was before Dave and I married. I'm also positive that I would not have become the person I am today had we not married. My desire is that when Dave and I encounter someone or something broken, as the reflection of Christ and the Church, we would (like Peter and John) in unity reach out with more than worldly wealth (silver and gold have I none). I pray that we would be able to say "Look at US!" and minister healing to an impossible situation. Find a way today (regardless of your stage of life) to celebrate your "one-ness".

Call to Love

Write a list of all the wonderful, considerate, and/or helpful things your spouse has done lately.

Find a way to show your gratitude and celebrate those things openly so that your spouse is uplifted.

Do nothing out of selfish ambition or vain conceit. Rather, in humility value others above yourselves, Not looking to your own interests but each of you to the interests of the others.

-(Phillipians 2:3-4, NIV)

15
Love is a Battlefield

Love is a Battlefield . . . marriages face challenges from two sides; within and without. On the within side, we have two individuals at various stages of growth/maturity living together, with strengths and flaws, trying to figure out life. Each of us makes mistakes and often those mistakes end up affecting our spouse. We experience growing pains and do not always handle those gracefully. One benefit of raising children is that I have had a front row seat to watching an incredible amount of growth (and response to the growth process) up close and personal.

Since we have four, I have also been able to see a variety of ways that a person can respond to the discomfort of growth. One is extremely introverted, another who is moderately extroverted, the third with special needs, and also an extreme extrovert. The first three were born very close together and have journeyed very closely as siblings. Our youngest was born 10 years after the others and is like raising an only child. Adding to the distance, the closest in age is on the autism spectrum. Response to growth, stress, and discomfort in our home range from self isolation to temper tantrums and explosions of anger, along with everything in between.

Raising little humans can put stress on a marriage, especially when you and your spouse disagree on what course of action to take as you attempt to guide their hearts through the phases of childhood and into adulthood - where hopefully they can take over and you can become a mentor and advisor (fingers crossed/folded in prayer). One thing I have learned about marriage and raising children: both are a matter of faith, trust, and prayer.

The sooner we relinquish the responsibility of holding onto the illusion that we are in control, the sooner we will be able to tap into the only truly qualified source for making decisions in our marriage and with our children. Let's face it, as adults, we ourselves are still growing and maturing. The best we can offer our children is based solely on what we have learned and experienced up to this point.

Aside from tapping into the fountain of the Holy Spirit's wisdom, the best we have to offer comes from the past. What we have for our spouse is an educated guess based on past experience.

The best we have for our children is also based on this past. If our past experiences are of the variety that we do not want our spouse and children to share, then we must look elsewhere.

"But as it is written, Eye hath not seen, nor ear heard, neither have entered into the heart of man, the things which God hath prepared for them that love him. But God hath revealed them unto us by his Spirit: for the Spirit searcheth all things, yea, the deep things of God. For what man knoweth the things of a man, save the spirit of man which is in him? Even so the things of God knoweth no man, but the Spirit of God. Now we have received, not the spirit of the world, but the spirit which is of God; that we might know the things that are freely given to us of God."
-(1 Corinthians 2:9-12, KJV)

When as a couple we come into unity based not on our personal need for control, but based on the revealed will of God we become fireproof in our marriage, operate from a position of peace and trust when raising our children, and weather the adversities of life without turning on each other and assigning blame.

Call to Love

Ask the Holy Spirit to give you;
-eyes that see,
-ears that hear,
-and a heart to understand,
the bigger picture and the greater purposes
He has for you and your spouse.

If applicable, add your children, and grandchildren in prayer or while meditating on this.

Speak words of life, hope, and peace into every situation.

In marriage there will be things that you do individually to keep life running, but the things that you build together will be the ones most fulfilling and most impactful.

16
Build This Thing Together

-Something to Consider

And, we can build this thing together . . . When God decided to create humankind in His own image and likeness, He created a "them" with Male & Female. First on a spiritual plane, with qualities that complement each other and when working in harmony result in life and creativity. The idea was for the Divine Trinity to open the "circle of divine unity" to a new member who would, like the Trinity, operate from oneness and so join the dance.

When husband and wife operate in the dance of oneness there is a give-and-receive, prefer-and-be-preferred exchange in which it is difficult to decide where one starts and the other ends. The journey of our marriage has been practicing and working out of a dance. This dance happens on multiple levels and in many different ways both big and small.

While our children were very little, we decided that it made more sense for me to stay home with our children and for Dave to work. Daycare for our three little blessings would have cost more than I would have earned in the current job market, and we both felt strongly about the importance of those preschool years in terms of natural and spiritual development. So, I stayed home to care for our children up until the youngest was school-aged. We had a newborn, a 16 month old, and an almost 3 yr old.

I remember one day Dave came home and found me on the couch with all three babies piled on me soundly sleeping. I sat there with numb arms and the TV remote. No shower yet, the house was a wreck, and I was literally trapped! I'm so thankful that Dave chose in that moment not to focus on the fact that the house was a mess, laundry was piling up, and dinner had not been started yet! Instead, he slowly peeled children off and put them down in their respective beds and sent me off to take a long soaking bath.

There is never an attitude between us "this is your responsibility" and "this is my responsibility". We have always divided up jobs (stuff gets done faster that way), both of us have viewed all responsibility as mutual responsibility. I must confess, there were days I wished to trade places with him. In those seasons I was learning to overcome my own tendency toward covetousness while gaining the ability to celebrate the little moments.

In marriage there will be things that you do individually to keep life running, but the things that you build together will be the ones that are most fulfilling and most impactful. There is a grace that comes from needing and relying on each other that brings depth and renewed intimacy to a relationship.

I remember transitioning our two oldest (Joy & Isaac) from toddler beds to a bunk bed. We lived in a two bedroom trailer at the time, so all three kids shared the larger of the two rooms. Dave and I worked together to assemble those bunk beds and bonded over the struggle. Neither one of us could have completed the job alone. Building your relationship is a lot like putting together bunk beds, it's the kind of job that requires both of you to lend your individual talents, strengths, and efforts while simultaneously leaning on the talents and strengths of the other. Both partners need to be willing to admit when you "don't got it", need a break, or do not understand what the other is asking/saying.

Whether cooking, painting, biking, hiking, or some other activity, find something that the two of you need each other to accomplish and make time to practice co-creating or co-accomplishing.

While there is no longer a need for bunk beds in our home, we still enjoy building and creating things together. Usually we cook together. Each of us has our "specialty" and then there are other things that either one of us makes reasonably well.

Call to Love

If you have been married for a while, think back on how your spouse has grown as an individual and as a partner.

Make a point to tell your spouse how proud and blessed you are to see all they accomplish.

When I have taken care of me, making love becomes a mutually beneficial and enjoyable activity, increasing our closeness. I am better able to both give and receive.

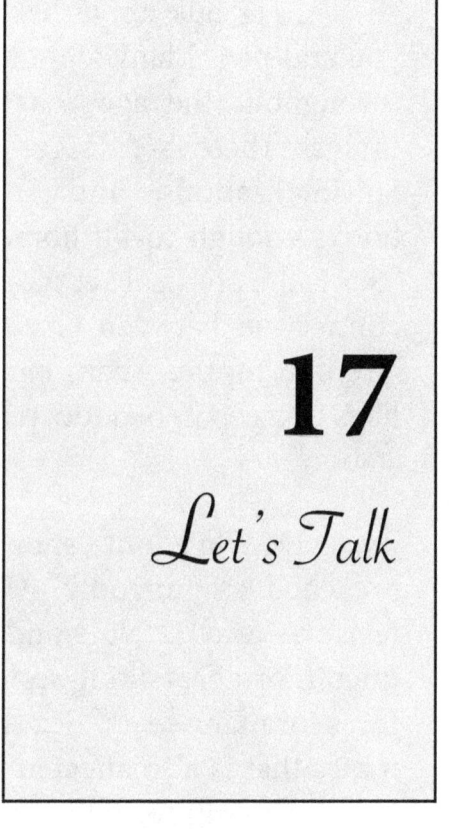

17
Let's Talk

-Something to Consider

Let's talk about sex, baby; let's talk about you and me! Many a book, spiritual and secular, throughout the ages has been written on the topic. There are "How Tos", "What to Not", Spiritualizations, and "Relationships & Sex" books enough to fill libraries. Everything from "Sex is the physical act that embodies the spiritual connection between Christ and the Church" to "It's putting the Adam back together". Legalism likes to creep in bed too, telling us what things are "taboo".

Denying our spouse sex is also been preached as "ungodly" (I'm sure the husband feels that way!). No wonder so many people are uncomfortable talking seriously about sex I know I was for many years. Sex seems to be one of those topics that is also affected by what I call the "Big Trifecta": culture, religion, and biology. Rarely do they all agree (unlike the Holy Trinity: Father, Son & Holy Spirit).

Western culture has shrouded human sexuality in both shame and sensationalism. Western Christian Culture has framed sexuality in shame and misogyny. Human biology has made the survival of the race dependent on sexual reproduction, and individuals (both male and female) fall on a broad spectrum when it comes to drive. If you want to learn about the "How Tos" this is not the chapter for you. I will touch on the subject of sex from a relationship point of view and share what I've learned.

The hope is in sharing you will come to your own realizations in your relationship. Each couple is unique. Both the beauty and the frustration of individuality (and freedom from legalism) as a couple is that you get to create (discover) your own "normal". The key is this has to be co-created. Realize, as well, that "normal" can/will change with age and life situations. Here is where our current social and spiritual culture of shame (at least the one I grew up in) and misogyny creates difficulties (especially for women, although men are not unaffected - remember, this is my point of view).

Before I get into sharing my perspective on how sex can either enhance your relationship or harm it, I need to lay down a few principles that have been established in our marriage. First, it is important for both of you to understand that no one "owes" anyone sex. Second, don't fall for the lie that you cannot control yourself and if one doesn't give you what the other needs "at a moment's notice" it is the other's fault if you go looking elsewhere. There is no room for selfishness in marriage, including the marriage bed. Self-control, the fruit of the Spirit, still applies after marriage. Just because the genie is out of the bottle and you've gotten a taste of the good stuff, it does not absolve you from being a decent human being.

Unfortunately, most of the time, it is the woman who is considered as being selfish or cold if she is "not in the mood". Heaven forbid should the man not be in the mood! The dart goes right for the juggler as his very manhood is questioned! The underlying message is that if she does not desire him physically at the time there is something wrong with him. Also (for the guys), if she does not reach orgasm then somehow he is under-performing, and again is not a good partner, let alone male. These messages of shame, which are directed to both men and women, work together breaking down communication, and creates a hot mess in the bedroom.

Now, I will speak as a woman, when our spouse gives us that "look", and you're not in the mood there is a choice to make: (1) Say "not tonight", (2) Try to work something up, or (3) fake it. Early in our marriage, my religious upbringing and cultural training told me that in order to be a "good wife" I had to be sexually available at least most of the time. Unless I was legitimately sick, or truly indisposed, my body belonged to him. I never talked about it with Dave and at the time I truly was not aware of what was going on, and honestly was too trained by shame to even know how to have the conversation. I thought, "love is sacrifice … it's like exercise, once you get going it's enjoyable and reaps benefits…basically: fake it 'til you make it!"

Culture and religion are that way. They shut down communication and prevent both growth and innovative solutions. It has always been easier for me to "deny myself" than have risky conversations. Culture and religions are hidden, fear-based systems of power imbalance that we have become so used to that we are not even aware they are there until something or someone challenges those beliefs.

Here's the problem, this type of mentality leaves one person feeling used. Sex becomes one more thing done to please, to keep the peace, and keep the relationship happy. Like laundry, dishes, or cooking dinner. Sure, both benefit from the laundry, dishes, and dinner as well, but it's still a chore. No matter how motivated you are to do these things out of love for the other, you are still spending energy by giving out. In order for this situation to not result in resentment, there must be some mutual benefit as well as some giving the spouse does that can refresh and replenish the other.

In my relationship with Dave, this means I need time alone to take care of myself. I need time out with my girlfriends where I can just be me. I wear a lot of hats: wife, mom, teacher, and minister. If I do not have a regular schedule of "hat-less-ness" then I start to loose myself and begin to resent everyone who "needs something from me", including my spouse.

Call to Love

Have an honest conversation with your spouse about where you are in your sexual relationship.

Be open about these interactions.

A healthy sexual relationship should be an enjoyable form of communication and interaction.

So they are no longer two, but one flesh. Therefore what God has joined together, let no one separate.

18
Help...
Is a Two Way Street

-(Mark 10:8b-9, NIV)

Help is a two-way street. One-sidedness is a relationship killer. Whether household responsibilities, raising children, or any number of the complicated interactions that make up a marriage. There must be equity, mutual trust, and respect. You both certainly bring unique strengths to the partnership. Keep in mind, just because an area is one person's strength does not mean that assistance is never needed, or that a new perspective should be ignored.

One of the side-effects of long term relationships is familiarity. It is easy to just assume you know exactly what your partner will say, think, or want simply because of past experience. Making these assumptions, though, does not allow for personal growth and is actually an ego-centric ploy for controlling others, preventing them from growing.

Depending on circumstances and life-seasons, our needs change over time. Everyone falls into routines, has favorites, and can get into a rut. Sometimes we don't even realize that our needs are changing or have changed until we notice dissatisfaction rising. When we notice our needs changing it is important not only to make them known explicitly, but also to give our partner time to adjust to the "new normal".

On that thought, part of the privilege we have as partners is that we get to encourage one another to try something new/different and take appropriate risks. Even after 20-plus-years of marriage, I do not allow myself to assume that I know how Dave feels or thinks about a given situation. I do not hold him to past thoughts, feelings, or actions because he has my permission (and encouragement) to grow, change, and evolve. I honor his right to grow by seeking to get to know him every day. I ask questions even when I think I know the answer because I value his journey.

When I said "I do", I did not sign up for a lifetime together with the same person I married 21 years ago. I signed up for a journey of becoming together. When we refuse to allow our partner to grow and change we hold them and the relationship hostage with our fears and insecurities. The people we are now (both individually and as a couple) are not the same people we were then. Our love has evolved, matured, and changed over the years. Our likes, dislikes, needs, and interests are different as well.

Embracing marriage is about embracing change and uncertainty. It's about choosing to trust that no matter how much you both grow, mature, and change the commitment is to evolve together. You allow your relationship to be reborn at every stage of the journey. Each day you decide to become the best version of yourself, and receive your partner as growing into their best version as well. You turn, time and time again, to one another for stability, belonging, and love.

Make a point today, this week, and always to sincerely ask for your partner's opinion. Recognize and communicate your own changing needs. Don't assume they know what you are feeling and/or thinking. Be patient to communicate more than once and in different ways. Repeated communication only becomes nagging when it is either communicated or received with negative emotions (e.g. annoyance or frustration). Never allow yourself to assume you know what is on his/her mind. Ask, and then listen as s/he shares with you. Make sure you notice and affirm him/her and re-commit to learning, growing, and evolving together.

Call to Love

Develop the mindset, in which those moments your spouse (or yourself) behaves in a disappointing fashion, that it is not reflective of who they are.

Realize and allow for out-of-character responses to pressure, stress, and growth pains.

I urge you to walk in a manner worthy of the calling, with all humility and gentleness, with patience, bearing with one another in love.

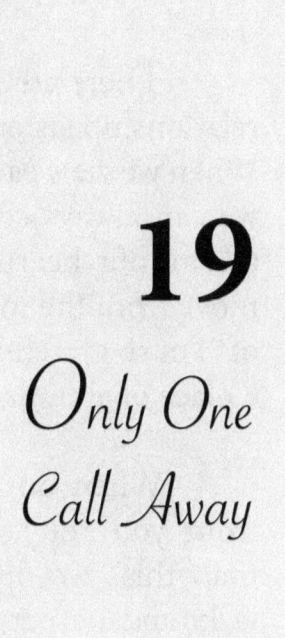

19
Only One Call Away

- (from Ephesians 4:1-3 NIV)

"I'm only one call away, I'll be there to save the day. Superman's got nothing on me. I'm only one call away."

There are very few things that revitalize a relationship faster than gratitude and admiration. When we view each other as "my hero", the person we can always count on to rescue, support, and affirm, our hearts are filled with gratitude. We move from the mentality of "you owe me" to one of "I'm so grateful". This is what I call living from a place of abundance.

When our life view is "I expected more from you" or "you should know/do/be better than this" we operate from a place of scarcity, lack, and perpetual disappointment. It appears that the very nature of religion and our current culture is immersed in attitudes of scarcity. We are constantly bombarded with messages of "not enough", "too much", and "should haves".

When someone shares about an experience they enjoyed, and we were not a part of, a sense of "you missed out" tries to bubble up. This mentality could seep into our marriage when our spouse behaves in a way that does not fit with our expectations, is out of the norm, or offends us (even if it not acknowledged or known to us at the time).

Whatever our preconceived ideas of what is "common sense" or "obvious", we must recognize that this line of thinking is counter-productive. It plays into our wounds, insecurities, and sets our relationships up for failure.

Conversely, if we have a mentality of gratitude, we increase the resilience of our relationship when the inevitable faux pas, miscommunication, or outright acts of selfishness happen. An attitude of scarcity responds to blunders, accusing the offender of intentionally hurting them or requiring that they "pay" or be "punished" in some way.

Each individual and personality manifests differently. Culture also plays a role in how we deal with offense and disappointment. Some common scarcity reactions include yelling, arguing, the silent treatment, gossiping/complaining to our friends, avoidance, and the like. The attitude of abundance responds with the assumption that offense was not intended, that was out of the norm, seeks to understand, and forgive.

Both attitudes still communicate that an offense took place. Ignoring or explaining away behaviors that hurt you only leads to a laundry list of complaints when the dam finally does burst (usually over something minor). The difference lies in that the attitude of scarcity tends to blame and punish; the attitude of abundance tends to communicate in order to educate, understand, bring about healing, and restore whatever has been damaged.

Honesty is difficult because it requires risky vulnerability. It requires that the offended person recognize that there is no need for blame. Blame is pointless. For the sake of healing and restoration, the offended must identify with the offender. We must resist the urge to say "I would never ..." and realize that We have been guilty of offending others, being selfish, and committing thoughtless deeds. As such an attitude of abundance, with compassion, understanding, and forgiveness are within reach. The abundance attitude says "we are all human and have permission to grow, you and our relationship are more important than this temporary pain."

Past experiences may also make the risk seem too great to take. You may have to be strategic so that you can grow toward greater levels of abundance mentality, reducing the scarcity mentality that has developed. It's important to have honest conversations about where you are in the journey out of scarcity as you head toward abundance.

Call to Love

Ask the Holy Spirit to reveal to you what areas of your life and marriage are being affected by the attitude of scarcity.

Address those areas with gratitude and the revelation that you are enough: made in the image and likeness of God.

Speak words of abundance and gratitude about your marriage, your spouse, and (if you have them) your children.

I waited patiently for the LORD; he turned to me and heard my cry

20
Waiting on You

-(Psalm 40:1 NIV)

Sitting at one of my favorite restaurants for a quick getaway, I'm reflecting back on the crazy week that I've had. Nearing the end of another school year teaching bi-lingual elementary and my brain is fried. I am feeling the effects of the toll that teaching can take mentally and emotionally.

Whether we like it or not, we carry all of life with us into our relationships. When we are tired, overwhelmed, when it feels life is not living up to our expectations, or are in the middle of the uncertainty of transition, tempers can flare and we can say or do things that are hurtful to others. Psalm 131:2 in The New American Standard Bible says: "*Surely I have composed and quieted my soul; Like a weaned child rests against his mother, My soul is like a weaned child within me.*"

As a mother to four children, I remember the seemingly incessant, continual cry of my babies when they were wet, hungry, or otherwise uncomfortable. There was no waiting. No patient pleasantness. There was only the screaming cry of demand. Human beings must be taught how to wait. Unfortunately, at least in my case, I only learned how to wait in a "socially acceptable manner". In other words, I stopped making all that racket externally, but internally I was still impatient. This was especially the case in times of personal discomfort.

Our fast-paced, have it your way, consumer society does not help matters. We add our impatient nature to our expectations and blend in a little stress and ¡viola!, the fighting ensues. However, in the last ten years I have begun to practice quieting and weaning my inner child. You can call it ego if you like. The result has been a greater peace within myself, a deeper connection with Dave, and greater joy raising our children.

Externally, my actions really haven't changed much; however, my emotional health has benefited. That in turn enhanced our entire family. Maybe I'm just lucky to have married such an awesome guy, but I've discovered that most of the issues in our marriage really traced back to my own need for personal growth.

I cause most of our problems, even when my husband's actions were inconsiderate, selfish, or immature. My response really did determine whether we had a problem or opportunity to communicate and improve.

Call to Love

When we wait for, wait on, and prefer our spouses patiently (internally & externally), we confer on them a deeper sense of love and honor. We enrich the relationship by valuing the other above self.

Today, take a moment to practice calming your inner-child (ego) through prayer, meditation, and Bible study.

If you've never learned these skills, take time to investigate them. Start training your soul to be composed and quiet.

But at the beginning of creation God 'made them male and female.' 'For this reason a man will leave his father and mother and be united to his wife, and the two will become one flesh.'

21
Reminiscing

- (Mark 10:6-9 NIV)

Reminiscing... It's a holiday weekend and I am feeling nostalgic. Really I've been nostalgic for a while now, reminiscing over both good memories and regretful ones, but mainly good. I've come to learn that those choices, attitudes, and behaviors that I regret now were actually great tools in God's hands. They exposed lies I believed about God, myself, and others.

Maybe I am reminiscing because I am reaching the end of these 21 devotions. Maybe it is because the school year is almost over and next year will be very different than this one. I will be teaching in a new building and with a new teaching partner. Maybe it is because our second child is graduating from high school this week, and about to begin the transition into adulthood. Maybe I am sensing the beginning of a new season.

Perhaps it is all of it combined ... and something more just beyond the grasp of my mind, but every present in my heart. The latter is most likely. My autistic son and I are the only ones awake. He's not much of a conversationalist, happy to have his food and play/replay videos on his tablet, so I made him breakfast and sat down to see if I can write some of the swirling thoughts on my mind.

My to-do list is long, and so many things on it are "finalizing this and finalizing that". Packing up my classroom, college orientation for our oldest son, and guardianship decisions for Ben. As it is a holiday weekend, I feel it is fitting to remember and reflect. Our busy, hurried, life leaves little room to stop and truly notice what we are experiencing in the mad, rushed passage of time. We are driven to move forward taking each event as it comes. Leaving the previous behind like a trail of litter in the wake of a toddler. "Git-er-done!"

"Now when all the nation had finished crossing the Jordan, the LORD spoke to Joshua, saying, "Take for yourselves twelve men from the people, one man from each tribe, and command them, saying, 'Take up for yourselves twelve stones from here out of the middle of the Jordan, from the place where the priests' feet are standing firm, and carry them over with you and lay them down in the lodging place where you will lodge tonight."

-(Joshua 4:1-3)

Often we underestimate the degree to which we are shaped by our past experiences. Significant events happen and we feel them deeply in the moment. They are seemingly monumental for a while. Then time passes, life happens, and we seemingly move on. We think we have forgotten them, their effects are over and we are now immune to the mark they have laid on our lives.

The children of Israel had a deep history of generational slavery in Egypt and a recent, but fraught history of their journey out of slavery and through the desert. It would be easy for all that history of shame, powerlessness, struggle, and death to overshadow the foundational experience of a peaceful entrance into God's blessings.

Though is was not the Red Sea crossing, the Jordan River crossing was just as miraculous. The waters still parted, but this time only stones were revealed. No armies were chasing at the "crossing over point" this time, no pillar of fire fending off the enemy while blocking all other choices. Though there would certainly still be battles, nothing was forcing them forward.

So, what does this have to do with marriage? Actually, everything! We are shaped by our past.

Both victories and struggles have brought us to where we are today; however, we get to choose which stones to take out of our crossing over. We get to decide whether to stay where we are, or enter into a new unknown. Like Joshua, we are the leaders of our lives and we get to decide what we will bring with us into our "new land of inheritance". We do this first individually, then as a couple.

When God spoke to Joshua, He told him to take a representative from each tribe to choose a stone for the memorial. As a couple, we must choose our "stones" and find a way to build our collective memorial. You will be both pleased and amazed how well both your sets of stones fit together and balance one another.

Remember, the same God who has been working in your life has also been working in your spouse's life, and your children's lives.

Call to Love

What will we memorialize as a reminder of who we are and where we are going?
Individually?
As a couple?
As family?
As a community of faith?

What legacy will we leave for our children and grandchildren?

Take some time to reflect. Real time and real reflection. Remember those things that have shaped you.

What stones will you carry with you?

www.ingramcontent.com/pod-product-compliance
Lightning Source LLC
Chambersburg PA
CBHW021956290426
44108CB00012B/1086